AT A CROSSROADS

AT A CROSSROADS

Between a Rock and My Parents' Place

Kate T. Williamson

Princeton Architectural Press, New York

Published by
Princeton Architectural Press
37 East Seventh Street
New York, New York 10003

For a free catalog of books, call 1.800.722.6657.
Visit our web site at www.papress.com.

Design: Kate T. Williamson
Editing: Clare Jacobson
Production: Arnoud Verhaeghe
Cover design: Deb Wood

Special thanks to: Nettie Aljian, Sara Bader, Dorothy Ball, Nicola Bednarek, Janet Behning,
Kristin Carlson, Becca Casbon, Penny (Yuen Pik) Chu, Russell Fernandez, Pete Fitzpatrick,
Wendy Fuller, Jan Haux, John King, Nancy Eklund Later, Linda Lee, Laurie Manfra,
Katharine Myers, Lauren Nelson Packard, Jennifer Thompson, Paul Wagner, and
Joseph Weston of Princeton Architectural Press —Kevin C. Lippert, publisher

Library of Congress Cataloging-in-Publication Data
Williamson, Kate T. (Kate Tower), 1979–
  At a crossroads : between a rock and my parents' place / Kate T. Williamson.—1st ed.
    p. cm.
  ISBN-13: 978-1-56898-714-9 (alk. paper)
  1. Williamson, Kate T. (Kate Tower), 1979– I. Title.
  PS3623.I569Z46 2008
  811'.6—dc22

                                                          2007029178

for my wonderful grandmother,

Dotty Williamson

After graduating from college and spending a year in Japan, I returned to Pennsylvania in September. My plan was to stay with my parents for three months while I worked on a book. It was nice to be home.

My bedroom—virtually unchanged since my childhood—was alternately comforting and unsettling.

personalized Lucite desk set

Being neat is berry sweet!

folder labeled "Disney World 1989"

contents:
autographed program from character breakfast
two coasters from Polynesian Resort Hotel

souvenir T-shirt collection

It is very pink.

My bathroom, also very pink

It was strange being home in September and not returning to school.

My parents' neighbors initially thought I was just visiting.

I wanted to finish the book, but I had a few other goals:

① Learn all the lyrics to Hall & Oates's <u>Rock 'n Soul Part 1</u>

② Clean my room

I rode my mother's bike to my grandmother's house every day to work on the book. I often cut through the school parking lot.

I worked on the book in my grandmother's "lower level." After a week of listening non-stop to Hall & Oates— excessive even for a fan— I found a method of receiving a weak NPR signal.

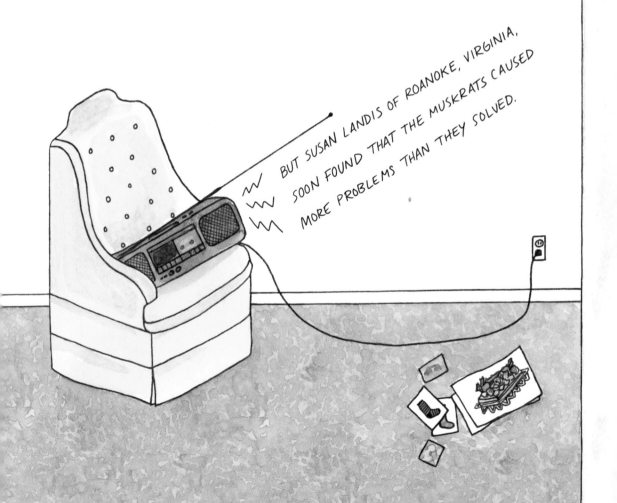

BUT SUSAN LANDIS OF ROANOKE, VIRGINIA, SOON FOUND THAT THE MUSKRATS CAUSED MORE PROBLEMS THAN THEY SOLVED.

WATERCOLOR

I became friends with the kids who live across the alley.

Some days we rode bikes together.

Other days I joined them for lunch.

Family Fun

on the Town

backseat: parents' friends and their son

at home

I was happy to be home to answer the door for the first time in many years. I wore my old college Halloween costume.

Keeping Busy

When I wasn't working on the book,

I worked part time as an SAT tutor

and danced on the weekends.

Sometimes I got very sad.

PARTY TIME!

By November, I was ready for a weekend away. My childhood friend invited me to a party at his apartment in New York City, and I eagerly accepted.

I sat down by the food table and did not move from my chair until 1 a.m.

when I relocated to a La-Z-Boy

and covered myself with an afghan.

At 3 a.m., I fell asleep on the coat bed.

I took the bus home the next day.

Thanksgiving

Each year, I am in charge of décor.

My chief duty is napkin folding. I usually fold the old standby, the fan, but this year I decided to spice things up with the bishop's hat.

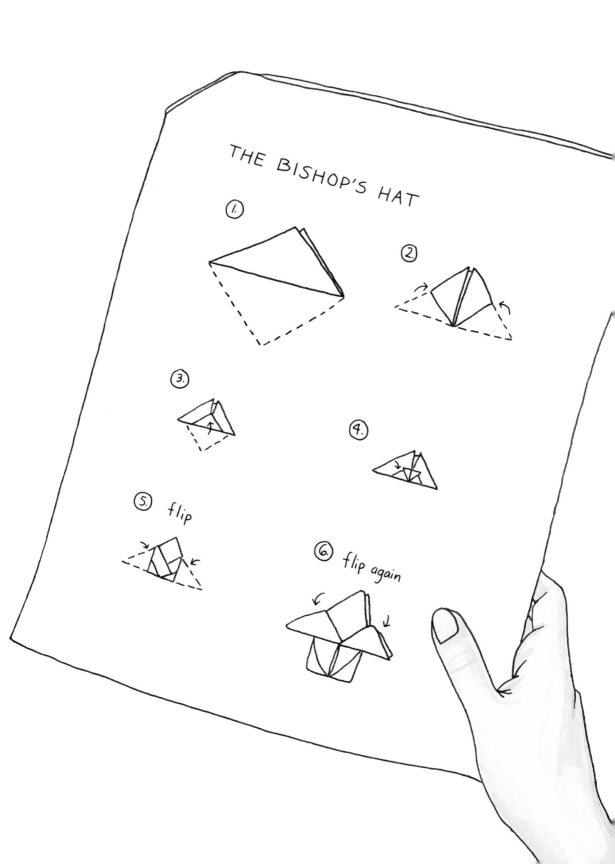

THE BISHOP'S HAT

1.

2.

3.

4.

5. flip

6. flip again

My social life picked up a little once I realized that two of my friends from high school were in town. Sometimes we went dancing at the nightclub in the Sheraton.

It was an older crowd.

We had a giant snowfall in December.

It was beautiful and still, a silence interrupted only by the occasional sound of an airplane or the wind.

New Year's Eve

FOR-EV-ER YOUNG!

I watched <u>Desperately Seeking Susan</u> until 11 p.m., when I switched to "Dick Clark's New Year's Rockin' Eve."

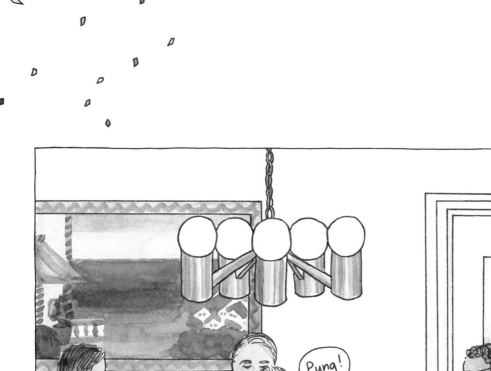

My parents played mah-jongg in the dining room with their friends. They joined me at midnight for nachos and a toast.

Self-Improvement

I started the new year by enrolling in what I thought was an adult ballet class. It turned out to be an intermediate children's class.

I was at least two feet taller than everyone in the class except
for an eighth-grader who, thankfully, was big for her age.
I think everyone assumed I was in ninth grade.

SQUIRREL TROUBLE!

For several nights in a row, I was awakened by what sounded like copulating squirrels.

As I suspected, squirrels had broken through the gutter guards that had recently been installed.

If I was quick, I could usually catch a glimpse of them.

I began to look forward to seeing the squirrels each morning.

Despite my concern for their fate, I eventually told my father about the squirrels. The gutter-guard people came the next day and, much to my relief, only banged on the gutter with a pole. Four squirrels ran out.

I am convinced that one of them gave me a reproachful stare shortly after its eviction.

HALL & OATES *LIVE!*

The highlight of my 24th birthday was seeing Hall & Oates in concert at the local theater. I was escorted by my mother.

Hall: the hunky one who sings all the songs

This is our latest single — right now it's #5 on the A.C. chart.

MANEATER!

From my seat in the back, Hall looked the same as he did in 1984. Oates, however, had shaved his moustache and cut his hair and sort of

After the show I lingered at the souvenir stand, where my mother dissuaded me from buying a "Maneater" baby T.

I was slowly making progress on the book. Sometimes I came upstairs during my grandmother's Friday bridge group for snacks and encouragement.

Spring

I really wanted my parents and grandmother to enjoy the cherry blossoms.

at the park

near my grandmother's condo

Easter
at my grandmother's house

My cousins brought the karaoke machine.

W.W.M.D. What Would Madonna Do?

There weren't many men between the ages of eight and forty in the neighborhood, so I was surprised to see my father talking to a cute guy one Saturday morning.

He turned out to be my nineteen-year-old neighbor.

When I asked myself what Madonna would do, I found an answer in Guy Ritchie, her husband ten years her junior. Still, I had reservations.

He also did not pass the Hall & Oates litmus test.

Although he was not a potential suitor,

I still tried to look cute while mowing the lawn.

Summer

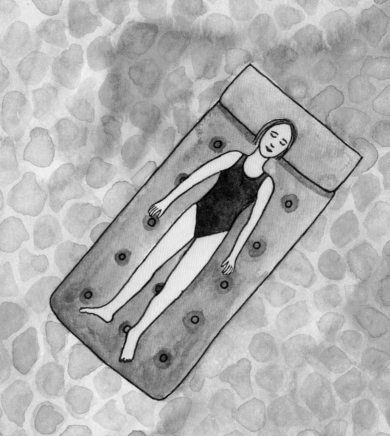

For two weeks in July, I was a live-in dog sitter for a sweet
Labrador retriever.

We both enjoyed her owners' pool.

I spent the evening of the Fourth floating in the pool and listening

to fireworks in the distance.

Polka Night

One Friday my friends and I decided to go to a minor league baseball game. My dad told me it was "Polka Night," so I thought it would be the perfect occasion to wear his old black lederhosen (purchased during a wild moment in the summer of '62 and subsequently handed down to me).

It turned out to be "Polish-American Night," and the only other people in costume were the four dancers on the field between innings. Although it was a doubleheader, I did not leave my seat until the end.

I felt a certain kinship with the man in a chicken suit performing "In the Air Tonight" in front of the food stands as we left the ballpark.

I liked listening to the buzz of cicadas.

Having spent the last two years of college pining away for a boy who did not share my feelings, I was excited to receive a letter from him in the mail. Was it possible he was confessing his love?

What followed was a detailed description of his first attempt at taxidermy.

In August I volunteered to be the scribe at my cousin's baby shower. My favorite gift was a doll that revolved while playing "Music of the Night."

I learned that another cousin would be having a
Renaissance-themed wedding in the spring. Costumes
were optional, but, after visiting some medieval websites,
I decided to start working on a chain mail miniskirt.

Autumn ... again

I could hear the trains from my room.

I never noticed them before.

After a full year of living at home, I detected some changes.
There were incipient signs of crotchetiness.

I found that my favorite songs on the radio tended to be playing on stations whose names began with "Easy," "Lite," or "Smooth."

In October, my father's barbershop chorus made it to the
mid Atlantic district championships, held in Wildwood,
New Jersey. I drove down there with him.

We arrived during the quartet competition. Four hours later, I began to amuse myself by coming up with names for imaginary quartets.

Barbershop quartet names seem to fall into three categories:

1. Suave
2. Macho
3. Vaguely Scientific

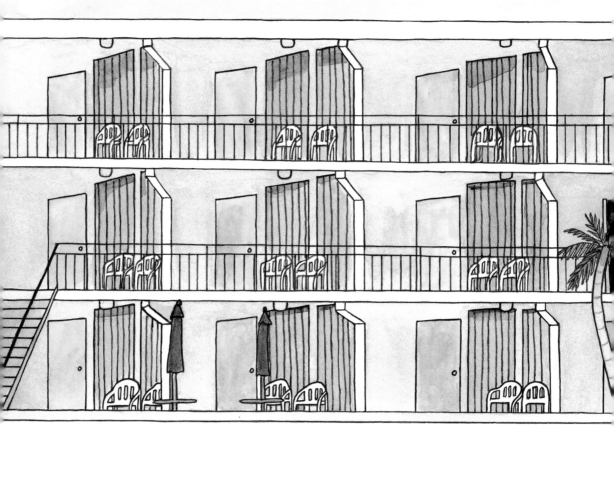

The fronds of Wildwood's fake palm trees had been removed
for the season and the trunks covered with plastic bags.

Only the Lu-Fran Motel left its palm trees intact. Rattling in the wind, they seemed cold.

Cher: Living Proof Farewell Tour

In late October, Cher came to town. I had no significant interest in seeing her until I heard a report on the radio the morning of the concert describing the eight tractor trailers that had just arrived carrying her sets and costumes.

Unfortunately, the show had been sold out for months. Undeterred, I got a ride with my friend's mother and hoped someone would be selling an extra ticket. Success crowned my efforts.

It promised to be an exciting show.

AT A CROSSROADS
epiphany

As I was searching for my seat, I looked up to see the mothers of two of my high school classmates. When they asked me what I was doing with my life, I was about to go through my song-and-dance about working on a book when it suddenly occurred to me to say that I was "at a crossroads." I was amazed that this, said while gazing off into the distance (in this case, toward the Cher JumboTron), quickly ended this line of questioning.

I had found the perfect response.

Home Haircutting

I decided I needed a change, so I gave myself bangs. Encouraged by the results, I tried cutting the side and soon realized I had gone too far.

I wore it tucked behind my ear for several days until my grandmother noticed and offered to even it out.

Update: **HALL & OATES**

While watching "CBS Sunday Morning" with my parents, I was excited to see a profile of Hall & Oates that answered many of my questions.

Oates: he <u>does</u> write a lot of the songs

Hall: currently single

HALLOWEEN II

I was not a plant this year.

At my mother's suggestion, I wore a blond wig and oversized sunglasses to answer the door until a surly trick-or-treater asked who I was supposed to be.

I muttered something about being a "movie star" (my
mother's idea) and then fled to the TV room, deaccessorized,
and spent the rest of the night watching <u>Bridget Jones's Diary</u>.

On the way to my grandmother's house, I passed the high school tennis courts, where gym class was occasionally in session. One day, I noticed a ball in the street and, trying to be helpful, heaved it into the middle of the court, where it hit an unsuspecting girl in the head. I felt compelled to change my route for several weeks.

SQUIRREL TROUBLE _redux_

After months without contact, the squirrels returned in November, this time above my bedroom at 2:35 a.m. They frolicked for a week before I told my father, who claimed they were merely on the roof. When I insisted these sounds seemed very close, he assured me they were the footsteps of mice.

The squirrels usually began their revelry after my father went to bed, but at last, weeks later, he heard them, too.

No action taken.

I decided to take matters into my own hands by mentioning the squirrels to my mother. My father, with a newly acquired sense of urgency, borrowed a Havahart trap and baited it with no-frills peanut butter. We waited.

My father claims that ever since Mr. Leisey, our ninety-seven-year-old, squirrel

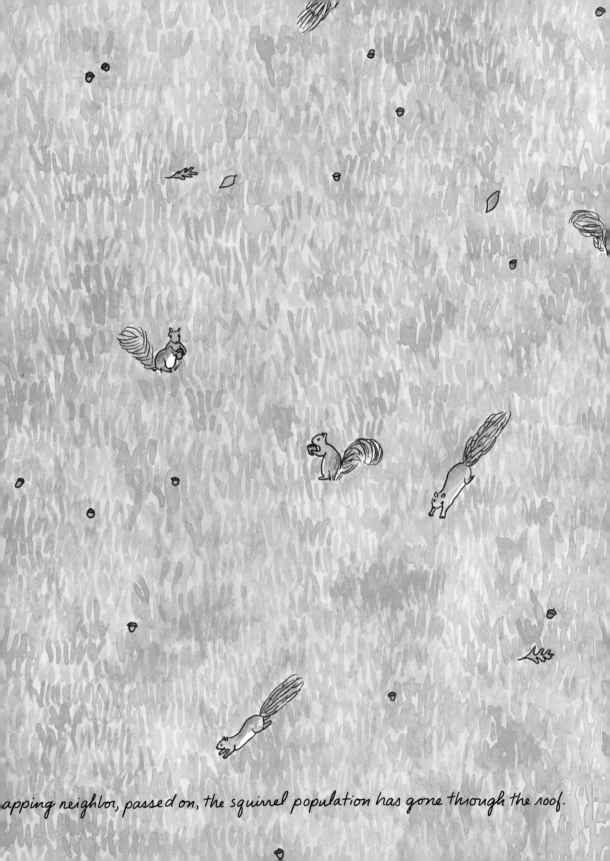

apping neighbor, passed on, the squirrel population has gone through the roof.

Sunday: the trap has been sprung.

Per Mr. Leisey's advice, my father released the squirrel
on the other side of a river.

On the way home, my father offered a career suggestion.

After warning me that I might not like this idea, he proposed that I paint portraits. I asked him whose portraits and, after some prodding, he revealed the plan.

I wasn't sure how to respond.

Chicago

the band, Christmas-style

Breaking my no Christmas-themed-anything-before-Thanksgiving rule, I went to hear Chicago perform their hits as well as songs from a new album of Christmas favorites ("Rudolph the Red-Nosed Reindeer" with a horn section).

I got a ride with my father's bookkeeper and her husband, who were celebrating their anniversary that night. (They met at a Halloween party where they danced to "Colour My World," which was also the first dance at their wedding.)

I had approximately the same seat I had for the Cher concert (very far away), but, unlike Cher, Chicago had no JumboTron, so they were very little.

Chicago: 24 songs, 4 fake trees
Cher: 13 songs, 1 fake elephant

By December, I had more or less finished my book.

I showed it mostly to relatives.

Then I sent it to publishers and waited.

I felt somewhat adrift.

The void of working on the book was soon filled with other activities. Years after shuffling through countless birthday parties (including my own), I decided it was time to learn how to roller skate.

I had my choice of rinks. Fantasy was farther away and smelled of Nibs; Jr. Skateaway had a scary turn in and out of the parking lot. I chose Fantasy.

I had a lesson Wednesday morning with the owner, Alan. To my surprise, I was the only one there at this hour. Alan put on half the disco lights and a tape of organ music.

the Flower Shop

I began working in a flower shop in December. This was a wonderful job. Since I had no experience, my floral duties were limited to making bunches and watering the potted plants.

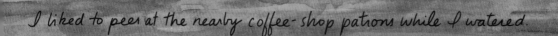

I liked to peer at the nearby coffee-shop patrons while I watered.

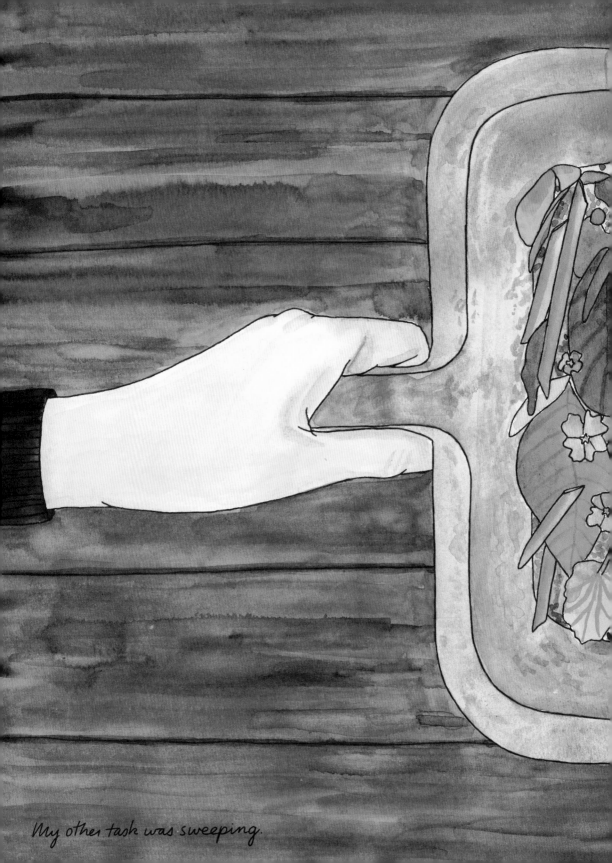

My other task was sweeping.

It is a popular flower shop, so I was constantly seeing people I vaguely knew.

Invariably, their children — my former classmates — were leading glamorous lives in big cities.

Sometimes I had to hide in the walk-in cooler.

the NOT-SO-FUNKY BUNCH

One of my earliest assignments as a bunch maker was to create a "presentation bouquet" for a woman whose daughter was graduating from art school. This seemed within my capabilities, so I began gathering "funky" flowers.

Things took a turn for the decidedly unfunky once miniature sunflowers got involved. Still, I thought it looked nice.

That night I lay in bed, haunted by the funky-lunch debacle.

Christmas Eve

The night before Christmas, I ran into an old Sunday school friend who had since moved away. I'm sure she meant well, but this was a particularly demoralizing exchange:

Back at the rink...

One Wednesday, I was alarmed to discover that, instead of the usual empty rink, there were about a dozen good skaters twirling about the floor. Alan explained that Jr. Skateaway had flooded and its skating club was practicing at Fantasy now. I was the only woman not in a skating skirt.

Valentine's Day

Valentine's Day Eve, not surprisingly, is a big night for the floral trade. Funky-bunch incident notwithstanding, I had been semipromoted to presentation-bouquet maker for customers who weren't very picky.

With spring came my cousin's Renaissance wedding in Seattle. I was embarrassed to be the sole passenger on the flight audibly amused by "Just For Laughs Gags."

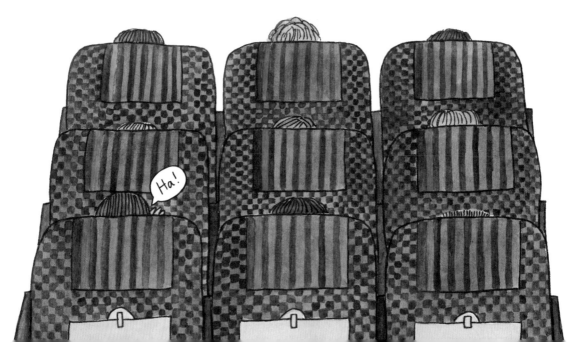

The fields below were beautiful and precise.

The chain mail "knitting" didn't go as quickly as planned — it was looking as though I'd have to show up in my seventh-grade Renaissance Faire costume — so I decided to cut my losses and make a belt.

The outdoor ceremony was lovely and involved lots of
trumpeting and swords. I was not the only guest in costume
(lots of cloaks and goatees).

I was now the only member of my extended family above the age of eight who did not have a car, cell phone, or significant other.

I went to the Pagoda (a "tea house" edged in neon lights that serves as my town's landmark, tourist attraction, and make-out spot) to think.

I listened to the _Paris, Texas_ soundtrack on my Walkman and vowed to stay until I came up with a plan for my life or my batteries ran out.

At 4:57 p.m. I saw a checkered sock in the sky.
I wasn't the only one to notice.

I decided I should move to New York City.

And then the lights came on.

Thank you

I am very grateful to my kind and patient parents, Judy & Jim Williamson; my dear friend Richie Williams; Constance Arauz; David Michael DiGregorio; Alison Zacharias; the Kuhn Family; Bethany Kreider; Stephanie Kahn; Tanya Leiby; Marci Clontz; Ching Han Wong; Rose Kahoza; Rachel Kovner; Julie Stump; Jenny Baer; Anne Estes; Vanessa Bertozzi; Mickey Duzyj; Rachel Salomon; Karen Acquista; Kim Beeman; Wendy Tilby; Susan Homer; Linas Alsenas; Heather Osterfeld; Ayano Ninomiya; Kattia Marquez; Owen Bossola; my thoughtful aunts; Suzy & Larry Daniels; Joan & David Andrews; Clare Jacobson, Kevin Lippert, and everyone else at Princeton Architectural Press; and the rest of my wonderful family and friends for their great support and encouragement.